Events o

News for every day of the year

Civilian defence volunteers in the Battle of Moscow

By Hugh Morrison

MONTPELIER PUBLISHING

Front cover (clockwise from left): US government poster commemorating the attack on Pearl Harbor. Ginger Rogers. German troops surrender to the Russians in the Battle of Moscow. British troops in Cyprus.

Back cover (clockwise from top): Inauguration programme for President Franklin D. Roosevelt. The USS *West Virginia* on fire after the attack on Pearl Harbor. A British soldier in gas training. Laurence Olivier and Joan Fontaine in *Rebecca*, which won an Oscar for Best Picture in 1941. The RAF's new Lancaster bomber. Rita Hayworth.

Image credits: Dr Indy, Matthew Straubmuller, Ralph PH, Rob Bogaerts/ Anefo, Boris Dzhingarov.

Published in Great Britain by Montpelier Publishing.
Printed and distributed by Amazon KDP.

ISBN: 9798630973405

Events of 1941

News for every day of the year

January 1941

Wednesday 1: 141 Royal Air Force bombers attack the Focke-Wulf aircraft factory near Bremen, Germany.

Thursday 2: Several German bombs are dropped on Dublin and other locations in neutral Eire; most likely due to navigational errors by aircraft attacking Northern Ireland.

The Andrews Sisters record *Boogie Woogie Bugle Boy.*

Friday 3: Bugs Bunny is named for the first time when he appears in the Looney Tunes short *Elmer's Pet Rabbit.*

Saturday 4: Allied forces seize the Italian-held town of Bardia in Libya.

Sunday 5: Aviation pioneer Amy Johnson is missing, presumed dead, after the RAF Air Transport Auxiliary plane she is piloting crashes off the Kent coast near Herne Bay.

Monday 6: US President Franklin D Roosevelt makes his famous Four Freedoms' speech in his State of the Union address.

Tuesday 7: Japanese forces draw up plans for war with the USA, proposing a crippling attack on the US fleet at Pearl Harbor.

The RAF Avro Lancaster heavy bomber goes into service on 9 January.

January 1941

Lord Baden-Powell.

**Joan Baez is born on
9 January.**

Wednesday 8: Robert Baden-Powell, former army officer and founder of the Scout movement, dies aged 83.

Thursday 9: The RAF's Avro Lancaster heavy bomber goes into service.

Folk musician and protest singer Joan Baez is born in New York.

Friday 10: German occupying forces in the Netherlands begin compulsory registration of Jews.

A US poll shows that 60% of American citizens are in favour of military intervention to assist Great Britain against German invasion.

Saturday 11: HMS *Southampton* is sunk near Malta during an Operation Excess supply convoy.

Sunday 12: British and Australian troops surround the Italian-held port of Tobruk, Libya.

Monday 13: 26 people are killed in a German air raid on Plymouth England.

Irish novelist and poet James Joyce (*Dubliners, Ulysses*) dies aged 58.

Tuesday 14: Actress Faye Dunaway is born in Bascom, Florida.

January 1941

Wednesday 15: RAF bombers raid Wilhelmshaven and Emden in Germany.

Thursday 16: The first German air raid takes place on the British colony of Malta in the Mediterranean, killing 50 people and destroying 200 buildings.

Friday 17: A record 23,190 spectators attend a boxing match in New York's Madison Square Garden, as Fritzie Zivic defends his world welterweight title against Henry Armstrong.

Saturday 18: A swastika flag is flown from the German consulate in San Francisco to celebrate the country's unification. Despite US neutrality, an angry crowd pulls down the flag and tears it to pieces.

Sunday 19: Troops of the Indian Army under General Platt together with the Sudanese Defence Force begin to drive the Italian army from Eritrea, British Somaliland and Ethiopia.

Above: the Inauguration of President Roosevelt.

Monday 20: The historic third inauguration of Franklin Delano Roosevelt takes place in Washington, DC.

Tuesday 21: The Bucharest Pogrom takes place in Romania.

January 1941

The communist newspaper *The Daily Worker* is banned in Britain due to anti-war propaganda.

The film *High Sierra* starring Humphrey Bogart and Ida Lupino is released.

Singer Placido Domingo is born in Madrid, Spain.

Wednesday 22: 25,000 Italians are taken prisoner as British and Australian forces capture Tobruk, Libya.

Left: British 'desert rats' advance on Tobruk.

Thursday 23: Charles Lindbergh testifies before the US House Foreign Affairs Committee claiming that America's proposed lend-lease programme for Britain violates US neutrality.

Singer Neil Diamond is born on 24 January.

Friday 24: The singer-songwriter Neil Diamond is born in New York.

Saturday 25: Diplomat William C. Bullitt warns the US House Foreign Affairs Committee that a German invasion of the USA is likely if the British fleet is destroyed.

Sunday 26: US politician Wendell Lewis Wilkie visits Britain as President Roosevelt's informal envoy, on a fact-finding mission to determine whether the USA should enter the war.

January 1941

Monday 27: Latin American countries meet in
Montevideo, Uruaguay, for a nine-day
conference on economic co-operation.

Tuesday 28: The British merchant ship *Urla* is
sunk by an Italian submarine off the coast of
Ireland.

Wednesday 29: Secret talks begin between
the US and British armies in Washington, DC,
to discuss plans for co-operation in the event
of the USA entering the war.

Joe Louis.

Thursday 30: In a speech made to a crowd of 18,000 people in
Berlin, Hitler warns the USA against entering the war, stating that
any ships giving aid to Britain will be attacked.

Friday 31: Boxer Joe Louis retains the World Heavyweight title
with a knock-out of Red Burman at Madison Square Garden, New
York City.

February 1941

Saturday 1: The Indian Army captures Agordat, Eritrea, and Metemma, Ethiopia.

Sunday 2: Southern Italy is declared a military zone and placed under martial law.

Monday 3: Erwin Rommel is appointed head of Germany's Afrika Korps.

President Batista takes over control of Cuba's armed forces.

Tuesday 4: The British merchant ship *Empire Engineer* is sunk in the north Atlantic by the German submarine U-107.

Wednesday 5: Luxembourg and Belgian's currency are replaced by the German Reichsmark.

HM King Alfonso XIII of Spain.

Thursday 6: Adolf Hitler makes a second unsuccessful attempt to persuade the neutral Spanish government to enter the war on his side.

Friday 7: British troops are victorious in the Battle of Beda Fomm in Libya.

Saturday 8: The US House of Representatives votes 265-165 in favour of the Lend-Lease programme of aid for Britain.

Actor Nick Nolte is born in Omaha, Nebraska.

Sunday 9: British Prime Minister Winston Churchill makes an international radio broadcast responding to the US

February 1941

end-Lease decision, stating 'give us the tools, and we will finish he job'.

Monday 10: German bombers attack British-held Iceland.

Tuesday 11: US diplomat Wendell Wilkie, returning from his fact-finding mission to the UK, urges Congress to provide the Royal Navy with at least five destroyers a month.

Above: Australian army nurses arrive in Singapore in preparation for Japanese attack.

The RMS *Queen Elizabeth* goes into service in Singapore as a troopship.

Wednesday 12: Spain's exiled King Alfonso XIII renounces the throne in favour of his son, the Infante Juan, Prince of Asturias.

Thursday 13: German authorities seal off Amsterdam's Jewish Quarter.

Friday 14: Britain announces that Romania will henceforth be considered an enemy state due to its co-operation with Germany.

Saturday 15: British and German troops engage for the first time in north Africa, as the Afrika Korps land near Sirte, Libya.

Sunday 16: North Korean leader Kim Jong-il is born in Vyatskoye, USSR (died 2011).

Monday 17: Greek troops defeat the Italian army at the Battle of Trebishina.

February 1941

Tuesday 18: The South African First Division captures Mega, Ethiopia.

Australian troops arrive in Singapore to bolster the colony's defences against Japan.

Wednesday 19: The three day Swansea Blitz begins in south Wales.

Thursday 20: The United States Coast Guard Reserve is established.

Friday 21: The Swansea Blitz in Wales ends with 230 people killed but no major damage to its docks and oil refineries.

Saturday 22: Britain agrees to send troops to aid Greece.

Sunday 23: HMS *Terror* is sunk off the north African coast.

Laurence Olivier and Joan Fontaine in *Rebecca*.

Monday 24: In a Gallup poll, 46% of Americans are opposed to the USA entering the war to protect British held Singapore from Japanese invasion.

Tuesday 25: A general strike begins in the Netherlands in protest against anti-Jewish laws of the occupying German forces.

British and South African troops capture Mogadishu, capital of Italian Somaliland.

February 1941

Wednesday 26: Eleven ships of North Atlantic Convoy OB-290 are sunk by German submarines.

Thursday 27: *Rebecca* wins Best Picture in the 13th Academy Awards. This is the first year in which the winners are announced from sealed envelopes.

Paddy Ashdown, leader of Britain's Liberal Democrat party, is born in New Delhi, India (died 2018).

Friday 28: The King of Spain in Exile, Alfonso XIII, dies aged 54.

March 1941

Saturday 1: Bulgaria signs the Tripartite Pact, joining the Axis powers.

Sunday 2: German troops reach the Greek border.

Monday 3: *Life* magazine publishes the famous photo of a Frenchman (left) watching in tears as the ceremonial colours (flags) of the army are hurried out of the country via the port of Marseilles to prevent capture by the Germans.

A man weeps as French flags are removed.

Tuesday 4: Adolf Hitler meets with the Prince Regent of Yugoslavia at Berchtesgarden to persuade him to enter the war on the Axis side.

In Operation Claymore, British commandos destroy 3,600 tons of oil and glycerine supplies in German-held Norway.

Wednesday 5: The drama series *Author's Playhouse* begins on NBC radio in the USA.

Adolf Hitler signs Directive Number 24, agreeing to co-operation with Japan.

Thursday 6: Artist Gutzon Borglum, creator of the Mount Rushmore Memorial, dies aged 73.

Friday 7: The second worst blizzard on record to this date hits New York City, with 18 inches of snow falling on Central Park.

March 1941

Saturday 8: The film *Footsteps in the Dark* starring Errol Flynn and Brenda Marshall is released.

Hugh Mulcahy of the Philadelphia Phillies becomes the first major league baseball player to be conscripted into the US army.

Sunday 9: A single German bomb is dropped on Buckingham Palace, London; it is one of 16 attacks on the palace during the war. The Royal Family are unharmed but a police constable is killed in the attack.

Police and bomb disposal experts with a defused bomb after Scotland's Clydebank Blitz.

Monday 10: Belgian Congolese troops seize the Italian held town of Asosa, Ethiopia.

France introduces beer rationing due to hop shortages.

Tuesday 11: US President Roosevelt signs the Lend-Lease act for aid to Britain.

Wednesday 12: President Roosevelt requests $7 billion in aid from Congress for the Lend-Lease programme.

Thursday 13: The two-day Clydebank Blitz begins as German bombers attack the ship-building area of Glasgow, Scotland.

Friday 14: Japanese and Nationalist Chinese forces clash in the Battle of Shanggao.

March 1941

Glenn Miller.

Saturday 15: *Song of the Volga Boatmen* by Glenn Miller and his Orchestra hits number one in the US charts.

Sunday 16: British forces recapture Berbera, capital of British Somaliland, from the Italians.

Monday 17: 162 German bomber planes attack the city of Bristol in south west England.

President Roosevelt opens the National Gallery of Art in Washington, DC.

Tuesday 18: Singer and songwriter Wilson Pickett is born in Prattville, Alabama.

The Luftwaffe attacks Liverpool and Birkenhead in north west England.

Wednesday 19: Hitler gives Yugoslavia an ultimatum to join the Axis forces within five days or face invasion; the country capitulates on 24 March.

Thursday 20: British troops seize Hargeisa in Italian-occupied British Somaliland.

Friday 21: Hungary's Foreign Minister, László Bárdossy meets with Adolf Hitler in Munich for war talks.

Saturday 22: Vichy France announces plans to build a trans-Saharan railway using Jewish and political prisoner labour. The project is abandoned in 1944.

Sunday 23: The British armed merchant vessel HMT *Visenda* sinks German submarine U-551 in the North Atlantic.

March 1941

Monday 24: Paul Green and Richard Wright's play *Native Son*, produced by Orson Welles, opens on Broadway.

Tuesday 25: The British ocean liner SS *Britannia* is sunk by German action off the coast of Brazil.

Wednesday 26: Rioting and demonstrations take place across Yugoslavia in protest against the government entering the war on the German side.

The British biologist and outspoken critic of religion, Richard Dawkins, is born in Nairobi, Kenya.

HM King Peter II of Yugoslavia

Thursday 27: Adolf Hitler orders the invasion of Yugoslavia, following a British-supported coup to prevent the country entering the war.

Friday 28: Following Yugslavia's coup, British-educated Prince Peter of Yugoslavia becomes King aged just 17.

Test pilot Hanna Reitsch becomes the first woman to receive Germany's Iron Cross.

Left: Hanna Reitsch receives the Iron Cross from Adolf Hitler.

March 1941

Virginia Woolf, author of novels including *Mrs Dalloway* and *To The Lighthouse*, commits suicide on 28 March.

British writer Virginia Woolf commits suicide aged 59 by drowning herself in the River Ouse; her body is not discovered until 18 April.

Saturday 29: *Amapola (Pretty Little Poppy)* by Jimmy Dorsey and his Orchestra tops the US charts.

Sunday 30: The British liner *Umona* is sunk off the coast of Sierra Leone by German submarine U124.

Monday 31: Following an incident in which a group of Jehovah's Witnesses blocked sidewalks, the US Supreme Court rules in Cox v New Hampshire that freedom of speech does not include the right to obstruct pedestrians for the purpose of evangelism.

April 1941

Tuesday 1: The RAF drops the first 4,000 pound bomb (known as a 'blockbuster') of the war on Emden, Germany.

The pro-British government of Iraq is overthrown in a military coup and replaced by a regime sympathetic to Germany.

Wednesday 2: The British pro-Nazi propagandist known as 'Lord Haw Haw' reveals his true identity as William Joyce in a radio broadcast. He is eventually captured and hanged for treason in 1945.

Thursday 3: The British army captures Asmara, capital of Eritrea.

Friday 4: German and Italian forces seize the port of Benghazi in Libya.

Saturday 5: British railway engineer Sir Herbert Nigel Gresley, designer of the world's fastest ever steam locomotive *Mallard* (126mph), dies aged 64.

British troops guard the city of Tobruk in Libya.

Sunday 6: Yugoslavia and the Soviet Union sign a treaty of friendship; on the same day Germany invades Yugoslavia. German forces also begin the invasion of Greece.

Monday 7: Britain severs diplomatic links with Hungary over its pro-German stance.

The Belfast Blitz begins.

Tuesday 8: The last Italian forces in Eritrea are defeated, giving Britain complete control of the country.

April 1941

Wednesday 9: The Danish colony of Greenland becomes a protectorate of the USA in exchange for the right to build air and naval bases there.

Thursday 10: The Siege of Tobruk begins.

Friday 11: (Good Friday). Hungary invades Yugoslavia, seizing back territory taken as part of the Treaty of Versailles after the Great War.

The Road To Zanzibar starring Bing Crosby and Bob Hope is released.

English football legend Bobby Moore (shown here in 1969) is born on 12 April.

Saturday 12: Bobby Moore, the captain of England's victorious 1966 World Cup football team, is born in Barking, Essex (died 1993).

Sunday 13: (Easter Sunday). Pope Pius XII makes an Easter broadcast appealing for peace to both the Allied and Axis forces.

Monday 14: King Peter II of Yugoslavia flees the country as German troops capture the capital, Belgrade.

Tuesday 15: German troops capture Sarajevo, Yugoslavia.

200 Luftwaffe aircraft attack Belfast, capital of Northern Ireland.

Wednesday 16: The British destroyer HMS *Mohawk* is sunk by the Italian navy off the coast of Tunisia.

Thursday 17: Yugoslavia formally surrenders to the Axis forces.

April 1941

British big band star Al Bowly, 43, (*Midnight, and the Stars and You*) is killed during an air raid in London.

Popular singer and bandleader Al Bowlly is killed during a London air raid.

Friday 18: 80 Axis prisoners of war escape in a mass breakout from Angler prison camp in Ontario, Canada; all are eventually recaptured.

Saturday 19: 34 firemen and women are killed when Poplar fire station, east London, is bombed. It remains the largest single loss of life in British fire brigade history.

Weightlifter Steve Sanko makes three successive lifts totalling a record 1000 pounds in York, Pennsylvania.

Sunday 20: The Battle of Athens: RAF and Luftwaffe fighters clash over Greece in a last-ditch attempt by the Allies to save the country from German invasion.

Actor Ryan O'Neal is born in Los Angeles, California.

Monday 21: Greece surrenders to Germany.

Tuesday 22: 72 civilians are killed in a direct hit on an air raid shelter in Plymouth, south west England.

Actor Ryan O'Neal (shown here in 1968) is born on 20 April.

April 1941

Wednesday 23: Following Greece's capitulation, the country's government and King George II flee to the island of Crete.

Thursday 24: Classical guitarist John Williams is born in Melbourne, Australia.

Friday 25: Adolf Hitler orders the invasion of Crete.

Saturday 26: The South African army captures 4000 Italian prisoners at Dessie in Ethiopia.

Sunday 27: The British destroyers *Diamond* and *Wryneck* are sunk by German action off the coast of Greece. German troops march into the Greek capital, Athens.

Monday 28: The singer and actress Ann-Margret, known as 'the female Elvis' is born in Valsjobyn, Sweden.

Tuesday 29: 8,000 Allied troops surrender to the Germans at Kalamata, Greece.

Wednesday 30: The collaborationist Greek government under Georgios Tsolakoglou, known as the Hellenic State, is set up.

Greek troops in retreat before surrender on 23 April.

May 1941

Thursday 1: Orson Welle's film *Citizen Kane* premieres in New York City.

The American breakfast cereal Cheerioats (later renamed Cheerios) is launched.

Friday 2: The Anglo-Iraqi war begins as British troops begin the battle to retake the protectorate from pro-Nazi forces.

Saturday 3: Italy annexes part of Slovenia, creating the Province of Llubljana.

Emperor Hailie Sellassie (seated) with British officers during the liberation of Ethiopia.

Sunday 4: British troops seize the city of Basra in Iraq.

Monday 5: The exiled Emperor Hailie Sellassie returns in triumph to liberated Ethiopia, exactly five years after it was occupied by Italian forces.

Tuesday 6: Iraqi forces retreat after suffering large losses in clashes with the British near RAF Habbaniya.

Wednesday 7: The German weather ship *München* is captured by the Royal Navy off the coast of Iceland; it contains secret documents which help the British to crack German codes.

Thursday 8: British and Transjordanian forces attack Rutbah Fort in Iraq.

May 1941

An Enigma decoding computer in use. The German military codes were thought unbreakable until a machine was captured.

Friday 9: A 21 year old Royal Navy officer, Lt David Balme, finds by chance an intact Enigma decoding machine when boarding a stricken German U-boat off the coast of Greenland, thus helping the Allies decode many secret radio messages.

Saturday 10: Germany's deputy *Führer,* Rudolf Hess, flies to Scotland in a secret unofficial attempt to broker peace with the Allies. He is imprisoned for life and dies in 1987 in suspicious circumstances, officially ruled to be suicide.

Sunday 11: Eric Burdon, lead singer of The Animals (*The House of the Rising Sun*) is born in Newcastle Upon Tyne, England.

Rudolf Hess.

Monday 12: The German government announces that Rudolf Hess is 'suffering from mental illness', and the position of deputy *Führer* is abolished.

Tuesday 13: Singer Ritchie Valens, who dies along with Buddy Holly and the 'Big Bopper' in a plane crash in 1959, is born in Los Angeles, California.

Wednesday 14: The first major internment of Jews in Paris takes place as 3,700 are arrested and sent to holding camps.

May 1941

Thursday 15: The British government makes an ambiguous statement on the visit of Rudolf Hess to Scotland on 12 May, in order to keep Germany guessing about what he has told them.

Friday 16: 52 people are killed when the British passenger ship Archangel is bombed by the Luftwaffe in the North Sea.

Saturday 17: King Victor Emmanuel III of Italy and the Albanian Prime Minister Shefqet Verlaci narrowly escape death when their car is fired at by an assassin in Tirana, Albania.

Sunday 18: Italy's Prince Aimone is declared King Tomislav II of Italian-annexed Croatia.

Monday 19: The Italian army in Africa's last stand at the mountain stronghold of Amba Alagi in Ethiopia ends in Allied victory.

German paratroopers land on Crete.

Tuesday 20: German paratroopers land on the Greek island of Crete in the first major airborne invasion in history.

Wednesday 21: A German submarine forces the passengers of neutral American ship SS *Robin Moor* to disembark into lifeboats and then sinks the vessel, causing an international incident and outrage in the USA.

Thursday 22: HMS *Fiji, Gloucester* and *Greyhound* are sunk following German air attack off the coast of Crete.

May 1941

Friday 23: World heavyweight boxing champion Joe Louis retains his title in a bout with Buddy Baer at Griffith Stadium, Washington DC.

Saturday 24: The Royal Navy's 'invincible' battlecruiser HMS *Hood* is sunk by the German battleship *Bismarck* in the Battle of the Denmark Strait, causing a large loss of morale in Britain.

Singer-songwriter Bob Dylan is born in Duluth, Minnesota.

Sunday 25: Girondins ASP defeats SC Fives 2-0 in the *Coupe de France* soccer final.

Royal Navy and Fleet Air Arm officers and ratings decorated for sinking the *Bismarck*.

In the backround is a Fairey Swordfish torpedo plane.

Monday 26: Royal Navy and RAF aircraft hunt down the German battleship *Bismarck*; the ship is badly damaged after a torpedo hit from a Fairey Swordfish plane and is scuttled the next day.

Tuesday 27: Despite slowing the German advance, British officers declare Crete to be indefensible and begin evacuation.

Wednesday 28: Vichy France and Germany sign the Paris Protocols granting Germany use of French bases in its colonies.

May 1941

Thursday 29: The Germans capture Chania, Crete's second largest town.

Friday 30: Floyd Davis and Mauri Rose win the Indianapolis 500. It is the last time the winning car employs two different drivers and the last race held until 1946.

Saturday 31: British forces are victorious in the Anglo-Iraqi war following the capitulation of the pro-German government.

Davis and Rose's winning car from the 1941 Indy 500, now in the Indianapolis Motor Speedway Museum.

June 1941

Sunday 1: The remaining Allied troops on Crete surrender; about 500 soldiers remain in hiding to assist partisans in resistance efforts.

Clothes rationing begins in the UK.

Monday 2: The Rolling Stones' drummer Charlie Watts is born in Kingsbury, London.

Tuesday 3: German troops massacre 180 civilians in reprisals over resistance attempts at Kandanos, Crete.

Charlie Watts: born on 2 June.

Dame Myra Hess.

Wednesday 4: The former Emperor of Germany, Kaiser Wilhelm II, dies in exile aged 82.

Thursday 5: Despite its neutrality, the USA grants use of 1000 marines to relieve the British garrison on Iceland so that troops can be deployed elsewhere.

Friday 6: Pianist Myra Hess is made a Companion of the British Empire in the King's Birthday Honours after becoming famous for her morale-boosting piano recitals in London's National Gallery.

Saturday 7: Golfer Craig Wood wins the US Open.

Sunday 8: Operation Exporter, the Allied invasion of Vichy French territory in Syria and the Lebanon, begins.

Monday 9: Australian forces defeat Vichy French troops in the Lebanon at the Battle of the Litani River.

Tuesday 10: The Indian Army's 15th Punjab Regiment captures Assab in Ethiopian from the Italians.

June 1941

Wednesday 11: The RAF begins a 20 day bombing campaign of Germany's Ruhr and Rhineland regions.

Thursday 12: Adolf Hitler meets with Romania's leader Ion Antonescu in Munich for war talks.

Friday 13: *Tom, Dick and Harry* starring Ginger Rogers, Phil Silvers and Burgess Meredith is released.

Saturday 14: The US government freezes all German and Italian assets in the USA. Croatia enters the war on the Axis side.

Sunday 15: The English Anglo-Catholic mystic and pacifist writer Evelyn Underhill dies aged 65.

Monday 16: As all German consulates in the USA are closed, British Prime Minister Winston Churchill announces that Britain and the USA's 'hands are joined across the oceans'.

Ginger Rogers stars in *Tom, Dick and Harry*.

Tuesday 17: Operation Battleaxe, the British attempt to break the siege of Tobruk, ends in failure with 1000 Allied casualties and the loss of almost 100 tanks.

Wednesday 18: Boxer Joe Louis retains the World Heavyweight title when he knocks out Billy Conn in the thirteenth round at the Polo Grounds stadium, New York City.

Thursday 19: All US consulates in Germany and Italy are ordered to be closed by the Axis powers.

June 1941

Friday 20: A Russian archaeological team in Samarkand discovers the tomb of the medieval Mongol warlord Timur or Tamerlane.

Saturday 21: Archibald Wavell is dismissed as commander in chief of the Indian Army and Allied forces in the middle and far east. He is replaced by Claude Auchinleck.

Claude Auchinleck.

German troops cross the USSR border.

Sunday 22: In the early hours of the morning, Germany begins its monumental invasion of the USSR, codenamed Operation Barbarossa, thus betraying the Nazi-Soviet Pact of the first two years of the war. This colossal act of hubris marks the beginning of Hitler's downfall.

Monday 23: Adolf Hitler arrives at the 'Wolf's Lair', the highly fortified headquarters for the invasion of the USSR on the Soviet-Polish border.

Tuesday 24: German troops capture the cities of Kaunus and Vilnius in Lithuania.

Wednesday 25: A five-day massacre of Jews begins in Kaunus, Lithuania.

Thursday 26: The technicolor film *Blossoms in the Dust* starring Greer Garson and Walter Pidgeon premieres in New York City.

June 1941

Friday 27: Hungary declares war on the USSR.

Saturday 28: German forces capture Minsk, the capital of Belarus.

Harlan F Stone is confirmed as the 12th Chief Justice of the USA.

Sunday 29: Germany is victorious in the Defence of Brest Fortress, the first major engagement in the invasion of the USSR.

The evacuation of children from Leningrad in the USSR begins.

Monday 30: German troops beat back the USSR's defensive forces in the Battle of Brody on the Soviet border.

July 1941

Tuesday 1: The first commercial TV service in the USA begins from NBC in New York City; CBS begins broadcasting one hour later.

Wednesday 2: *CBS Television Quiz*, the world's first regular live TV quiz show, is broadcast in the USA.

Thursday 3: 290,000 Soviet troops surrender to the Germans near Minsk, Belarus; the USSR's leader Joseph Stalin appeals on the radio for all citizens to fight with all possible means.

Friday 4: German troops push further east, crossing the Dniepr River in Belarus.

Heinrich Himmler inspects Soviet POWs in Minsk.

Saturday 5: 254 servicemen are killed when the British troopship *Anselm* is sunk in the Atlantic by German submarine U-96.

Sunday 6: A monument to legendary baseball player Lou Gehrig is unveiled at the Yankees Stadium in New York City. He died from a neuromuscular illness, later named Lou Gehrig Disease, on 2 June.

Lou Gehrig.

Monday 7: Soviet leader Joseph Stalin is not reassured by Winston Churchill's offer of help from Britain in the war against Germany, and calls for a formal treaty.

Comedian and ornithologist Bill Oddie (*The Goodies*) is born in Rochdale, England.

July 1941

Tuesday 8: American journalist Richard C. Hottelet is released from jail in Germany, after serving a four month sentence on suspicion of espionage.

Wednesday 9: Questions are asked in Parliament about the pro-German propaganda broadcasts being made by expat British comic writer P.G. Wodehouse in Berlin to the USA. Wodehouse's reputation is seriously damaged and he never returns to Britain after the war.

William and Brenda Holden

Thursday 10: The ragtime and jazz musician Jelly Roll Morton dies aged 50.

Friday 11: The British destroyer HMS *Defender* is sunk by German action off the north African coast.

Saturday 12: British and Russian forces sign the Anglo-Soviet Agreement in Moscow.

Sunday 13: Hollywood star William Holden marries Brenda Marshall near Las Vegas, Nevada.

Monday 14: Vichy French forces formally surrender to the Allies in the city of Acre in British Palestine, ending the war in the near east and bringing Syria and the Lebanon under British control.

Tuesday 15: The German army captures the city of Yartsevo in the Battle of Smolensk.

Wednesday 16: Soviet leader Joseph Stalin's son, Yakov Dzhugashvili, is captured by the Germans.

July 1941

Thursday 17: Virginia Woolf's final novel *Between the Acts* is published posthumously.

Friday 18: British and Australian commandos destroy Italian supply lines in the 'Twin Pimples Raid', hampering the Axis efforts to take Tobruk.

Saturday 19: Italy's General Ettore Bastico is appointed Commander in Chief of Axis forces in north Africa.

Sunday 20: British leader Winston Churchill refuses Stalin's demands for the opening of a western front in Europe.

The BBC begins its 'V for Victory' campaign, appealing to occupied Europe to chalk the letter V on walls.

General Douglas MacArthur.

Monday 21: The first German air raid on Moscow takes place.

Tuesday 22: Songwriter and music producer George Clinton is born in Kannapolis, North Carolina.

Wednesday 23: The British destroyer HMS *Fearless* is sunk by Italian aircraft off the coast of Algeria.

Thursday 24: German and Romanian troops seize back the territories of eastern Romania previously ceded to the USSR.

Friday 25: Japanese and Chinese assets in the USA are frozen.

Saturday 26: General Douglas MacArthur is appointed commander of US forces in the Far East.

Composer Dmitri Shostakovich in the uniform of a Leningrad auxiliary fireman.

Sunday 27: The German army captures 100,000 prisoners at Smolensk.

Monday 28: Actress Judy Garland marries songwriter David Rose.

Tuesday 29: Russian composer Dmitri Shostakovich is photographed on duty as a volunteer fireman in Leningrad. The pictures are published around the world as a symbol of Soviet determination.

Wednesday 30: German troops reach Kiev in the Ukraine.

Singer Paul Anka is born in Ottawa, Canada.

Thursday 31: The four-week-long Ecuadorian-Peruvian War ends in a ceasefire.

August 1941

Friday 1: The US government announces an embargo of oil exports to any country in the western hemisphere outside the British Empire.

Saturday 2: All civilian owned radios are confiscated by occupying German forces in Norway.

Sunday 3: US TV personality Martha Stewart is born in Jersey City, New Jersey.

Monday 4: Adolf Hitler meets with senior generals to discuss the taking of Moscow.

Tuesday 5: The First Battle of Smolensk ends with German victory; 310,000 Soviet troops are taken prisoner.

Wednesday 6: In the British parliament, the Foreign Secretary Anthony Eden warns Japan against any invasion of Thailand.

Thursday 7: US President Franklin D. Roosevelt and British Prime Minister Winston Churchill meet for secret war talks on board the USS *Augusta* at Placentia Bay, Newfoundland.

Ace pilot Douglas Bader is shot down and captured on 9 August.

August 1941

Friday 8: German forces begin the Siege of Odessa in the Ukraine.

Saturday 9: The legless British ace pilot Douglas Bader is shot down over occupied France and taken prisoner by the Germans.

Sunday 10: US President Roosevelt and Britain's Prime Minister Winston Churchill attend a joint US/UK church parade on board HMS *Prince of Wales* in Newfoundland. Churchill himself chooses the hymns, which include *O God Our Help in Ages Past.*

Above: Rita Hayworth.

Below: Father Maximilian Kolbe.

Monday 11: The iconic 'pin up' of film star Rita Hayworth wearing a negligee is published for the first time in *Life* magazine.

Tuesday 12: Vichy France bans political parties and a introduces a compulsory oath of loyalty for public officials to the President.

Wednesday 13: The German government announces that all property belonging to Jews is to be confiscated.

The womens' army corps in Australia and Canada are founded.

Thursday 14: A Polish monk held in Auschwitz concentration camp, Father Maximillian Kolbe, is executed by the Germans after volunteering to exchange places with another prisoner, a family man sentenced to death after an escape attack. Kolbe is later canonised by the Roman Catholic Church.

August 1941

Churchill and Roosevelt at their historic meeting in Newfoundland on 10 August.

Friday 15: Josef Jakobs, a German spy arrested by the Home Guard after a botched parachute landing in Huntingdonshire, becomes the last person to be executed at the Tower of London.

Saturday 16: British TV antiques expert David Dickinson is born in Stockport, Cheshire.

Sunday 17: German troops capture the historic Russian city of Novgorod.

Monday 18: An obscure German record, *Lily Marleen*, begins to be played constantly on Radio Belgrade due to a lack of other records. The song becomes an instant hit with both Allied and Axis forces and is later re-recorded by Marlene Dietrich.

Tuesday 19: The British troopship *Aguila* is sunk in the Atlantic by German submarine U-201.

Wednesday 20: The second major round-up of Jews in Paris takes place, with 4232 arrested.

Thursday 21: The German army begins to surround the Russian city of Leningrad.

August 1941

Friday 22: Following the killing of a German officer in Paris by Resistance fighters, the German occupying forces announce that French prisoners will be shot if further such incidents occur.

Saturday 23: Adolf Hitler makes the fateful decision to delay the advance on Moscow until the city of Kiev is in German hands.

Sunday 24: The German programme of euthanasia for the physical and mentally disabled is officially ended due to public outcry but also a greater need for forced labour; many killings continue unofficially until the end of the war.

Monday 25: An assassination attempt takes place on Pierre Laval, Prime Minister of France. Laval is shot four times and narrowly evades death.

Tuesday 26: The Ukrainian city of Chernobyl, later infamous for its nuclear catastrophe, is taken by the German army.

Wednesday 27: The evacuation of Soviet forces from German-besieged Tallin, Estonia, begins. Known as the 'Russian Dunkirk', 165 ships are saved but at least 12,000 Soviets are thought to have died in the action.

Thursday 28: Around 23,600 Ukrainian Jews are murdered by German, Hungarian and Ukrainian units in a pogrom known as the Kamianets-Podilskyi massacre.

Friday 29: Public opinion turns against US neutrality campaigner Charles Lindbergh after he harshly criticises Britain, particularly with regards its administration of India.

Saturday 30: British commandos carry out Operation Acid Drop to kidnap German officers from Calais in occupied France, but fail to encounter any Germans.

Sunday 31: Yugoslav troops seize the German-occupied city of Loznica, which they hold until the Germans retake it in October.

September 1941

Monday 1: The first US TV station outside New York, KYW-TV in Pennsylvania, begins broadcasting.

Tuesday 2: Over 3,700 Jews are massacred by German and local police at Ponary near Vilnius, Lithuania.

Wednesday 3: The German army comes within artillery range of Leningrad, which it begins shelling.

Thursday 4: The New York Yankees win the American League baseball tournament with a 6-3 win over the Boston Red Sox.

Friday 5: German SS troops massacre 1500 Jews in Pavoloch, Ukraine.

Soviet troops guard Leningrad.

Saturday 6: Adolf Hitler orders the attack on Moscow for the end of September.

Sunday 7: A Gallup poll in the USA shows that 70% of Americans favour a check on Japanese expansionism, even if it risks war.

Monday 8: The Siege of Leningrad begins.

Tuesday 9: Following a successful invasion by British and Soviet forces, Iran comes under British control, thus safeguarding oil supplies for the war effort.

Singer Otis Redding is born in Dawson, Georgia (died 1967).

Wednesday 10: Martial law is declared in German-occupied Norway.

September 1941

Thursday 11: The Royal Navy destroyers *Leamington* and *Veteran* sink the German submarine U-207 in the Denmark Strait.

Friday 12: The collaborationist government of Norway bans the Boy Scout movement and replaces it with the pro-Nazi *Nasjonal Samling* organisation.

Orson Welles.

Saturday 13: 77 Norwegians are killed when the civilian ship SS *Baroy* is sunk by Allied action off the Norwegian coast. The ship was being used to transport German troops as well as civilians; the incident is seized on by the Germans for propaganda.

Sunday 14: Despite its neutrality, the US Navy provides escorts for the British North Atlantic convoy Hx50, the first direct US involvement in the North Atlantic campaign.

Monday 15: *The Orson Welles Show* premieres on CBS radio in the USA.

Adolf Hitler orders the German military rocket programme to be stepped up.

Tuesday 16: Reza, the Shah of Iran, abdicates in favour of his pro-British son, Mohammed Reza Pahlavi.

Wednesday 17: The German government makes listening to foreign radio stations a capital offence.

Thursday 18: The Soviet Union introduces conscription for all men aged between 16 and 50.

September 1941

Friday 19: The German army captures Kiev in the Ukraine.

Singer 'Mama' Cass Elliot of the Mamas and Papas is born in Baltimore, Maryland (died 1974).

Saturday 20: Three ships of North Atlantic Convoy SC44 are sunk by German submarines.

Sunday 21: The first German U-boats enter the Mediterranean Sea.

Monday 22: King George II of Greece arrives in exile in England.

Britain holds 'Russian Tank Week', a week in which all armoured vehicles produced are to be sent to Russia.

Tuesday 23: The Russian battleship *Marat* becomes the first battleship in history to be sunk by dive bombers, when it is attacked by German Stuka planes at Kronstadt, Russia.

HM King George II of Greece.

Wednesday 24: Representatives of the Allied countries meet at St James' Palace, London, for the Inter-Allied Council.

Thursday 25: The war film *A Yank in the RAF* starring Tyrone Power and Betty Grable premieres in the USA.

Friday 26: 1608 Jews are massacred by occupying German forces in Kaunus, Lithuania.

Saturday 27: British commandos carry out Operation Chopper, attacking targets in Normandy. Lithuania.

September 1941

Sunday 28: The first British convoy of supplies to northern Russia departs from British-occupied Iceland.

Monday 29: Boxer Joe Louis beats Louis Nova at the Polo Grounds stadium, New York City, to retain his World Heavyweight title.

Tuesday 30: Germany launches Operation Typhoon, the assault on Moscow.

Soviet anti-aircraft gunners in Moscow.

October 1941

Wednesday 1: The USA agrees to give $1 billion of military aid to the USSR.

Thursday 2: The Battle of Moscow begins. Ending in German defeat in 1942, it is the decisive battle of the entire Second World War.

Friday 3: The detective film *The Maltese Falcon* starring Humphrey Bogart as Sam Spade premieres in New York City.

Singer Chubby Checker, credited with inventing the 'twist' dance of the 1960s, is born in Spring Gully, North Carolina.

Saturday 4: The German submarine U111 is sunk off the island of Tenerife in the Atlantic by HMS *Shirley.*

Sunday 5: RAF bombers attack the German-occupied city of Prague, capital of Czechoslovakia.

Humphrey Bogart, Mary Astor and Peter Lorre in *The Maltese Falcon.*

October 1941

Tuesday 7: In order to boost morale and patriotism, Soviet leader Joseph Stalin lifts the ban on religion in the USSR.

Wednesday 8: A New Zealand farmer, Stanley Graham, kills seven people in a shooting spree including two police officers and two Home Guardsmen sent to arrest him. A major manhunt follows and Graham is eventually found and killed in a shoot-out on 20 October.

Thursday 9: Edourd Deladier, former Prime Minister of France, and other senior French politicians are indicted by the Vichy government for treason against the state.

Friday 10: The comedy film *Never Give a Sucker an Even Break* starring W.C. Fields premieres in the USA.

Saturday 11: The evacuation of all children and women not involved in war work from Moscow begins.

Sunday 12: Between 10,000 and 12,000 Jews are shot dead by German and Ukrainian troops at Stanislawow in eastern Ukraine.

Singer Paul Simon is born on 13 October.

Monday 13: The singer-songwriter Paul Simon of Simon and Garfunkel is born in Newark, New Jersey.

Tuesday 14: Italy's Chief of Defence Ugo Cavallero orders the invasion of the British colony of Malta in the Mediterranean.

Wednesday 15: With the Germans only 68 miles from Moscow, most of the Soviet government evacuates.

October 1941

US comic book characters Jughead (left) and Archie.

The teenage cartoon characters Archie Andrews and Jughead first appear in print in the USA.

Thursday 16: The Siege of Odessa in the Ukraine ends in Romanian victory. It is considered the most significant victory of any non-German Axis army in the war.

Friday 17: 11 US servicemen are killed when the destroyer USS *Kearny*, on defensive duties in Allied convoy SC48 near Iceland, is torpedoed by a 'wolfpack' of German U-boats. Hitler later uses the engagement as part of his justification for declaring war on the USA.

Saturday 18: Hideki Tojo becomes Prime Minister of Japan.

Sunday 19: As the German army encircles the Russian capital, Soviet leader Joseph Stalin declares a state of seige and announces that 'Moscow will be defended to the last.'

The USS *Kearny* showing torpedo damage on her hull.

October 1941

Monday 20: England test cricketer Ken Farnes is killed in an air crash in Oxfordshire while serving in the RAF.

Tuesday 21: The comic book superheroine *Wonder Woman* makes her first appearance.

Wednesday 22: 27 French hostages are shot by German authorities in reprisal for the killing of a German soldier by the Resistance.

Thursday 23: The Walt Disney cartoon *Dumbo* premieres in New York City.

Friday 24: A three day massacre by Axis authorities ends in Odessa in the Ukraine; up to 34,000 Jews and 15,000 gypsies are killed.

Maureen O'Hara in *How Green Was My Valley*, the story of a nineteenth century Welsh family, based on the novel by Richard Llewellyn.

Saturday 25: Bad weather halts the German advance on Moscow.

Sunday 26: Decorative chrome, nickel and aluminium are banned in US car manufacture.

Monday 27: F. Scott Fitzgerald's novel *The Last Tycoon* is published posthumously.

Tuesday 28: The John Ford-directed film *How Green Was My Valley*, starring Walter Pidgeon and Maureen O'Hara is released.

October 1941

Hideki Tojo becomes Prime Minister of Japan on 18 October.

Wednesday 29: British prime minister Winston Churchill makes his famous 'never give in' speech while visiting Harrow School, stating 'we have only to persevere to conquer'.

Thursday 30: US neutrality activist Charles Lindbergh addresses a rally of 20,000 people in New York City, claiming that Roosevelt is using subterfuge to draw the country into war.

Friday 31: The American convoy escort destroyer USS *Reuben James* is sunk with 115 hands by German action in the North Atlantic.

November 1941

The Rainbow Bridge opens on 1 November.

Saturday 1: The Rainbow Bridge connecting the USA and Canada at Niagra Falls is opened.

Singer Art Garfunkel is born on 5 November.

Sunday 2: A Vichy French convoy is captured by the Royal Navy off the coast of Madagascar.

Monday 3: The German army captures the Russian city of Kursk.

Tuesday 4: British politician Lord Halifax is pelted with eggs by isolationist demonstrators while visiting Detroit. He is said to have quipped 'in Britain we only get one egg a week' but this revealed as a press fabrication.

Wednesday 5: Singer Art Garfunkel of Simon and Garfunkel is born in Queens, New York.

Thursday 6: The first cases of frostbite begin to appear with German troops on the Eastern Front.

Friday 7: Bette Davis becomes the first female president of the Academy of Motion Picture Arts and Sciences.

November 1941

Frank Pick, designer of the London Transport logo and house style, dies aged 62.

Saturday 8: The Royal Navy knocks out several Italian supply ships in the Mediterranean's Battle of the Duisburg Convoy.

Joe DiMaggio kisses his bat.

Sunday 9: The German army occupies the city of Yalta in the Crimea.

Monday 10: In Operation Flipper, British commandos fail in their assassination attempt on Erwin Rommel, commander of German forces in North Africa.

Tuesday 11: Baseball player Joe DiMaggio of the New York Yankees is named the American League's Most Valuable Player.

Wednesday 12: British commandos make an overnight raid on Houlgate, France.

Thursday 13: The Royal Navy aircraft carrier HMS *Ark Royal* is torpedoed and severely damaged off the coast of Gibraltar; she sinks twelve hours later.

Friday 14: Alfred Hitchcock's thriller *Suspicion* starring Cary Grant and Joan Fontaine is released in the USA.

Saturday 15: The German army restarts its advance on Moscow despite temperatures falling to -20C (-4F)

Sunday 16: The Royal Navy's corvette HMS *Marigold* sinks German submarine U-433 off the southern coast of Spain.

November 1941

HMS *Legion* rescues the crew of the sinking HMS *Ark Royal*.

Monday 17: The Soviet army successfully defends the port of Murmansk from invasion in Operation Silver Fox.

Tuesday 18: Actor David Hemmings (*Blow Up*) is born in Guildford, Surrey (died 2003).

The British Eighth Army begins Operation Crusader, an attempt to break the siege of Tobruk.

Wednesday 19: The Australian ship HMAS *Sydney* is sunk by the German cruiser Kormoran off the western coast of Australia; Kormoran is badly damaged and later scuttled.

Thursday 20: US-Japanese diplomatic talks begin in Washington, DC; the Japanese demand that the USA halts naval build-up in the Pacific.

Friday 21: The British 70th Division breaks through the German lines at Tobruk.

Saturday 22: British commandos carry out an overnight raid on Houlgate, France.

Sunday 23: The British 7th Armoured Division is forced to withdraw after being outflanked by Axis forces at Sidi Rezegh.

November 1941

Monday 24: Pete Best, the original drummer with The Beatles, is born in Madras, India.

Tuesday 25: The first of two mass killings of Jews known as the Ninth Fort Massacres begins in Kaunus, Lithuania.

Wednesday 26: A Japanese strike force sets sail for Pearl Harbor, on the understanding that if peace talks with the USA are successful, it will be called off.

Thursday 27: The Siege of Tobruk ends in Allied victory as the garrison is relieved by the British Eighth Army.

Friday 28: The Palestinian nationalist leader Amin al-Husseini meets with Adolf Hitler in Berlin where each pledges mutual support.

Saturday 29: *Chattanooga Choo Choo* by Glenn Miller and his Orchestra hits number one in the US charts.

Sunday 30: Greta Garbo's final film, *Two Faced Woman* is released. Shortly afterwards she retires into reclusion and is rarely seen in public again.

Free Polish commander General Sikorski inspects troops after the Tobruk victory.

December 1941

The USS *West Virginia* on fire after the devastating surprise attack on Pearl Harbor by the Japanese on 7 December.

Monday 1: The United States Civil Air Patrol is formed.

Tuesday 2: The Moscow Defence Zone of heavy barricades around the city is set up, as German forces close in on the Russian capital.

Wednesday 3: The US Secretary of State Cordell Hull makes a pessimistic announcement about the US-Japanese peace talks, stating that a settlement is unlikely.

Thursday 4: The US government's top secret war plan, Rainbow Five, is leaked to the press, alarming isolationists.

Friday 5: Britain declares war on Finland, Hungary and Romania.

Saturday 6: In a letter to Japan's Emperor Hirohito, US President Roosevelt makes a last appeal for peace 'for the sake of humanity'.

Sunday 7: The Japanese surprise attack on Pearl Harbor begins at 07.55. 21 US ships are destroyed and 2418 US citizens are killed; Japan declares war on the USA and the British Empire.

December 1941

Monday 8: The USA and Britain declare war on Japan. In a speech to Congress, President Roosevelt says that 7 December is 'a date that will live in infamy.'

Tuesday 9: China, Cuba and Guatemala declare war on Japan.

Wednesday 10: Japanese forces close in on British possessions in the Pacific; HMS *Prince of Wales* and *Repulse* are sunk off the coast of Singapore and troops advance on Hong Kong.

Thursday 11: Germany and Italy declare war on the USA.

Friday 12: The Universal horror film *The Wolf Man* starring Lon Chaney Jr is released.

Saturday 13: On the Hawaiian island of Niihau, a downed and heavily armed Japanese pilot is killed while resisting arrest by unarmed local man Ben Kanahele, who is later awarded a Purple Heart for bravery.

Sunday 14: Japanese and Indian Army forces engage at the Battle of Gurun in Malaya.

Lon Chaney in *The Wolfman.*

Monday 15: A two day massacre of Jews and communists begins at Liepaja in Latvia by occupying German forces; 2754 people are killed.

Tuesday 16: Hitler orders 'fanatical resistance' in the Battle of Moscow and refuses to allow any retreat from the city.

Wednesday 17: Japanese forces invade Penang in the British colony of Malaya.

December 1941

Japanese troops enter the British colony of Hong Kong.

Thursday 18: The Japanese army invades Hong Kong.

The USA's Manhattan Project for the development of an atomic bomb begins.

Friday 19: The head of the German army, Field Marshal Walter von Brauchitsch, is relieved of command by Adolf Hitler who takes over personal control of all military forces.

Saturday 20: *Elmer's Tune* by Glenn Miller and his Orchestra hits number one in the US charts.

Sunday 21: The first episode of BBC radio's epic drama serial of the life of Christ, *The Man Born to be King* by Dorothy L. Sayers, is broadcast.

Monday 22: Winston Churchill arrives in secret in Washington, DC, for the Arcadia Conference on joint UK/US war plans.

Tuesday 23: In the face of overwhelming Japanese military superiority, General Douglas MacArthur declares the Phillipines' capital Manila an open city and evacuates to Bataan.

Wednesday 24: China defeats the Japanese army at the Battle of Changsha.

December 1941

Thursday 25: Despite heroic street-by-street resistance by its small defence force, many of whom are volunteer reserves or armed special constables, Hong Kong falls to the Japanese.

Comedy duo Olsen and Johnson.

Friday 26: The musical film *Helzapoppin'* starring Olsen and Johnson is released in the USA.

Saturday 27: British commandos carry out two raids on occupied Norway, Operation Anklet and Operation Archery.

Sunday 28: Rear Admiral Ben Moreel USN proposes the formation of the Construction Battallion (later known as the 'Seabees') to carry out military engineering projects.

Monday 29: The organisers of the Indianapolis 500 motor race announce the event's cancellation for the duration of the war.

Tuesday 30: In the Canadian Parliament, Winston Churchill responds to Vichy France's threat that Britain would have 'its neck wrung like a chicken' by saying 'some chicken – some neck!'

Wednesday 31: Footballer and Manchester United manager Sir Alex Ferguson is born in Glasgow, Scotland.

Admiral Chester Nimitz takes over the US Pacific Fleet.

Printed in Great Britain
by Amazon

66089004R00037